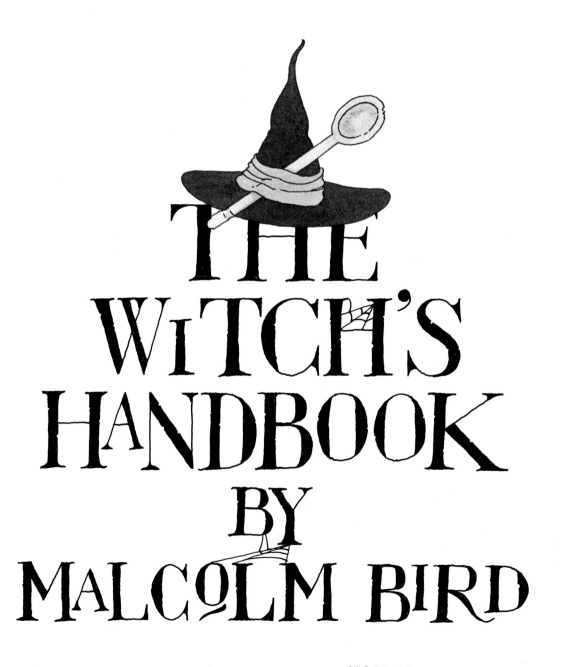

THE WITCH'S HANDBOOK

BY MALCOLM BIRD

THE WITCH'S HANDBOOK
BY MALCOLM BIRD

CHILDRENS PRESS CHOICE

THE AUTHOR AND PUBLISHERS WARN THAT THE PRACTICAL
INFORMATION CONTAINED IN THIS HANDBOOK MUST ONLY BE
USED BY FULLY-FLEDGED WITCHES AND THAT ANYONE ELSE
USING SUCH INFORMATION DOES SO ENTIRELY AT THEIR OWN
RISK.

Children's Press Choice, Chicago. 1987 School and Library Edition.
ISBN: 0-516-08460-7

Copyright © 1984 Malcolm Bird. First published in the U.S.A. in 1984
by St. Martin's Press. Created by A.K.A. Ltd Produced by David Booth
(Publishing) Ltd, 8 Cranedown, Lewes, East Sussex BN7 3NA
England. All rights reserved. Printed in Italy.

Library of Congress Catalog Card Number 84-52864

FOR ALAN

ACKNOWLEDGEMENTS
TO ALAN DART FOR ALL HIS
HELP WITH THE RECIPES AND
KNITTING PATTERNS, AND TO
MARGARET TARRATT AND
KEVIN GOUGH-YATES WHO
SUGGESTED THE IDEA AND SO
PROVIDED MANY HAPPY HOURS
DRAWING A FAVOURITE SUBJECT—
THANK YOU.

CONTENTS

CHAPTER 1
CHOOSING AND FURNISHING A HOME

SUITABLE HOMES

THE BAT TOWER
FOR THE WITCH WHO LIKES SLEEPING ALL DAY AND PLAYING WITH HER BAT FRIENDS ALL NIGHT.

STACKPOLE'S MILL
WITCHES LIKE ANYTHING THAT'S FREE, SO THIS MILL HAS BEEN CONVERTED TO PROVIDE FREE ELECTRICITY.

STOODLEY PIKE
SPECIALLY BUILT FOR A LAZY WITCH WHO CAN'T BE BOTHERED TO TAKE OFF HER HAT INDOORS.

THE TOLLHOUSE
IDEAL FOR A NAUGHTY WITCH WHO CAN MUDDLE CAR DRIVERS BY TURNING THE SIGNPOST ROUND.

UNSUITABLE HOMES

10 SUNNYSIDE STREET
A TERRACED HOUSE IS NOT SUITABLE FOR A WITCH AS NEIGHBOURS ARE INCLINED TO BE VERY NOSEY.

HONEYSUCKLE COTTAGE
THERE IS LITTLE PRIVACY IN A PRETTY COTTAGE AS IT INVITES A CONSTANT STREAM OF TOURISTS.

HOME FOR RETIRED WITCHES
WITCHES ARE SELFISH AND HATE TO SHARE ANYTHING, SO A HOME LIKE THIS WOULD NOT BE A SUCCESS.

A TENT ON EAGLE CRAG
THE PREVAILING WINDS MAKE THIS AN IMPRACTICAL PLACE TO LIVE —PICTURESQUE THOUGH IT IS.

THE PERFECT HOME

A WITCH'S HOME IS VERY IMPORTANT TO HER AND IT IS WHERE SHE PERFORMS HER MAGIC. THE WITCH HERE HAS BEEN MOST KIND IN ALLOWING PART OF THE WALL TO BE REMOVED SO THAT HER PERFECT HOME CAN BE SEEN MORE EASILY.

BROOMSTICK LAUNCH

BATHROOM

BAT ROOST

WOODSHED

KITCHEN

13

OUTDOOR POOL

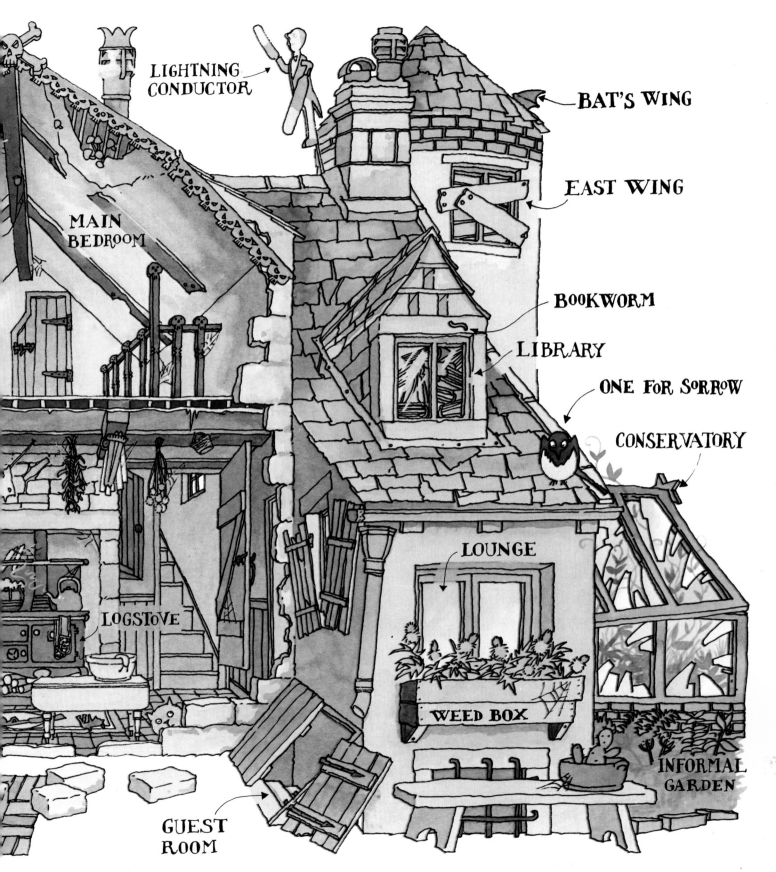

LIGHTNING CONDUCTOR

BAT'S WING

EAST WING

MAIN BEDROOM

BOOKWORM

LIBRARY

ONE FOR SORROW

CONSERVATORY

LOUNGE

LOGSTOVE

WEED BOX

INFORMAL GARDEN

GUEST ROOM

USEFUL FINDS

MUD PACK DISPENSER
KEEP A SPARE SINK FULL OF MUD

BROOMSTICK BOOSTER
FOR THOSE NO LONGER YOUNG

PASTRY MAKER
MIXES AND ROLLS OUT PASTRY DOUGH

BED SETTEE
TO DETER UNWELCOME GUESTS

IMPROVING FURNITURE

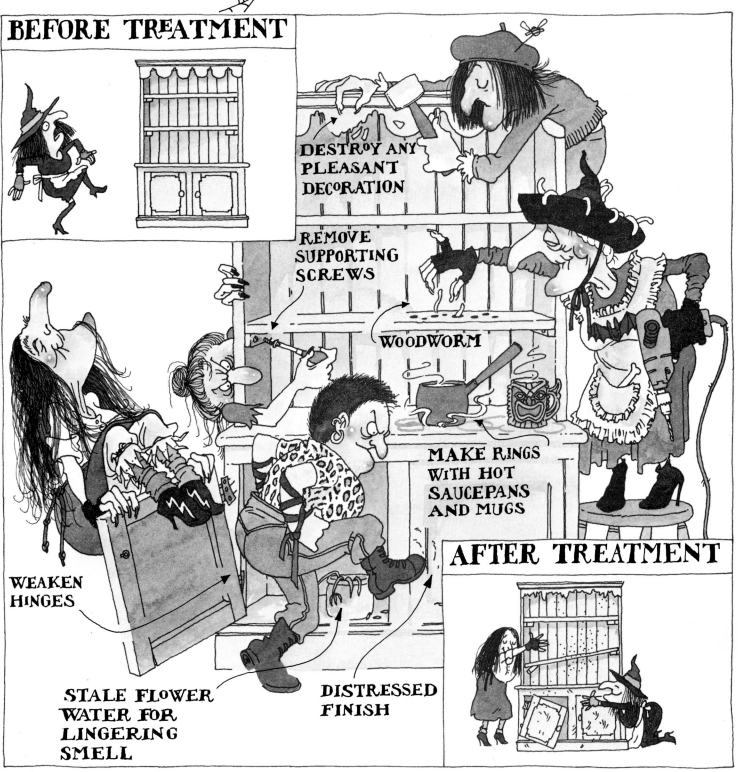

BEFORE TREATMENT

DESTROY ANY PLEASANT DECORATION

REMOVE SUPPORTING SCREWS

WOODWORM

WEAKEN HINGES

STALE FLOWER WATER FOR LINGERING SMELL

DISTRESSED FINISH

MAKE RINGS WITH HOT SAUCEPANS AND MUGS

AFTER TREATMENT

CHAPTER 2
THE WITCH'S KITCHEN

THE LARDER

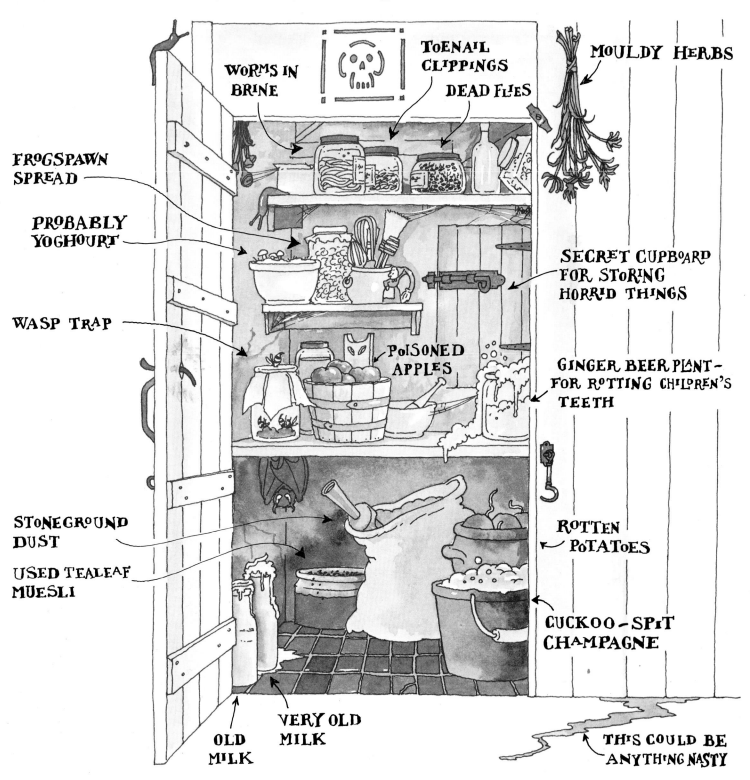

WORMS IN BRINE

TOENAIL CLIPPINGS

DEAD FLIES

MOULDY HERBS

FROGSPAWN SPREAD

PROBABLY YOGHOURT

WASP TRAP

SECRET CUPBOARD FOR STORING HORRID THINGS

POISONED APPLES

GINGER BEER PLANT - FOR ROTTING CHILDREN'S TEETH

STONEGROUND DUST

USED TEALEAF MUESLI

ROTTEN POTATOES

CUCKOO - SPIT CHAMPAGNE

OLD MILK

VERY OLD MILK

THIS COULD BE ANYTHING NASTY

KITCHEN EQUIPMENT

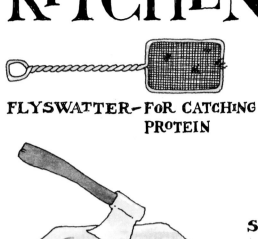

FLYSWATTER—FOR CATCHING PROTEIN

CUTLERY

BUN TRAY

TASTEFUL CROCKERY

CHOPPING BOARD

SIEVE—FOR SAVING THE CHEWY BITS

GERM-RIDDEN MIXING BOWL

STEWING PAN

CAULDRON

RUSTY SAUCEPAN

STALE BREAD DOUGH

BRAVE SPIDER

SMOKE—MEANS STOVE NEEDS CLEANING OR IS ON FIRE

FIREBOX

ASHPAN

CREOSOTE FROM BURNING GREEN WOOD

WARMING SHELF FOR TURNING MILK

KETTLE OF STEWED WATER

DAMPERS

RAIL FOR SCORCHING TEACLOTHS

OVEN

BURNT-ON FOOD

SOOT DOOR

WARM PLACE FOR LOGS AND PETS

LOGSTOVE

INGREDIENTS

SOME OF THE INGREDIENTS USED BY WITCHES IN COOKING ARE NOW DIFFICULT TO FIND AND ONLY VERY OLD WITCHES ARE STRONG ENOUGH TO DIGEST MOST OF THEM. ANYONE ELSE, ESPECIALLY HUMAN BEINGS, MUST USE THE SUBSTITUTIONS SHOWN BELOW.

INSTEAD OF WORMS..

USE SPAGHETTI CUT TO SIZE

INSTEAD OF DEAD FLIES..

USE CURRANTS AND RAISINS

INSTEAD OF HOUSEHOLD DUST..

USE GROUND GINGER

INSTEAD OF DRIED BEETLES...

USE LENTILS

INSTEAD OF TOENAIL CLIPPINGS..

USE FLAKED ALMONDS

INSTEAD OF POISONOUS TOADSTOOLS..

USE FLAT MUSHROOMS

KNEEBONES

THESE BISCUITS HAVE THE TEXTURE OF BONE — FOR CARNIVORES WITH A SWEET TOOTH

USING A CLEANISH BOWL...

·· MIX 4 OZ BUTTER WITH 12 OZ CASTOR SUGAR

BUTTER

CASTOR SUGAR

ADD ONE BEATEN EGG — THIS ONE DOESN'T SMELL TOO BAD.

ADD 2 HEAPED TSP GROUND GINGER ··

AND 9 OZ SELF RAISING FLOUR, THROUGH A SIEVE.

EGG

GINGER

FLOUR

MIX WELL FOR ABOUT 6 MINUTES — IF YOU'VE THE PATIENCE.

ROLL INTO 36 SMALL BALLS AND PLACE ON BAKING SHEET. BAKE AT 300°F * FOR 30 MINUTES.

NOW HIDE IN A CORNER AND EAT THEM ALL — THEY'RE TOO GOOD TO SHARE.

* Gas mark 2

DUSTBREAD BISCUITS

THESE SHOULD BE MADE WITH HOUSEHOLD DUST — BUT WHO'S GOT THE TIME TO SOAK DUSTERS AND THEN DRY OUT THE SCUM?....

SO IT'S MUCH EASIER TO SUBSTITUTE GROUND GINGER..

SO.. MELT 2oz MARGARINE, 4oz GOLDEN SYRUP, AND 2oz SUGAR TOGETHER OVER A LOW HEAT. ALLOW TO COOL.

← MARGARINE

SIEVE 12oz PLAIN FLOUR 1 TSP. GROUND GINGER AND ½ TSP. BICARBONATE OF SODA INTO A BOWL

FLOUR

GOLDEN SYRUP

IF THE SIEVE ISN'T CLEAN, IT WILL ADD TO THE FLAVOUR.

NOW ADD SYRUP MIXTURE AND ONE BEATEN EGG — AND MIX TO FORM DOUGH.

SUGAR

ICING

ROLL OUT TO ¼ INCH THICK

EGG →

USING TEMPLATES OPPOSITE, CUT OUT BISCUITS. EXCEPT FOR THE BONES, EACH BISCUIT NEEDS TWO SHAPES — ONE WITH FEATURES CUT OUT AND ONE WITHOUT.

PLACE ON GREASED TRAYS AND COOK FOR 15 MINUTES AT 400°F.* COOL ON RACKS.

SANDWICH TOGETHER WITH APPROPRIATE FILLINGS, AND DECORATE WITH ICING AS SHOWN

THE BONE ONES ARE QUITE BORING, SO YOU CAN EAT THEM AS YOU WORK.

← GINGER

* Gas mark 6

BICARBONATE OF SODA →

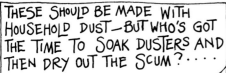

20

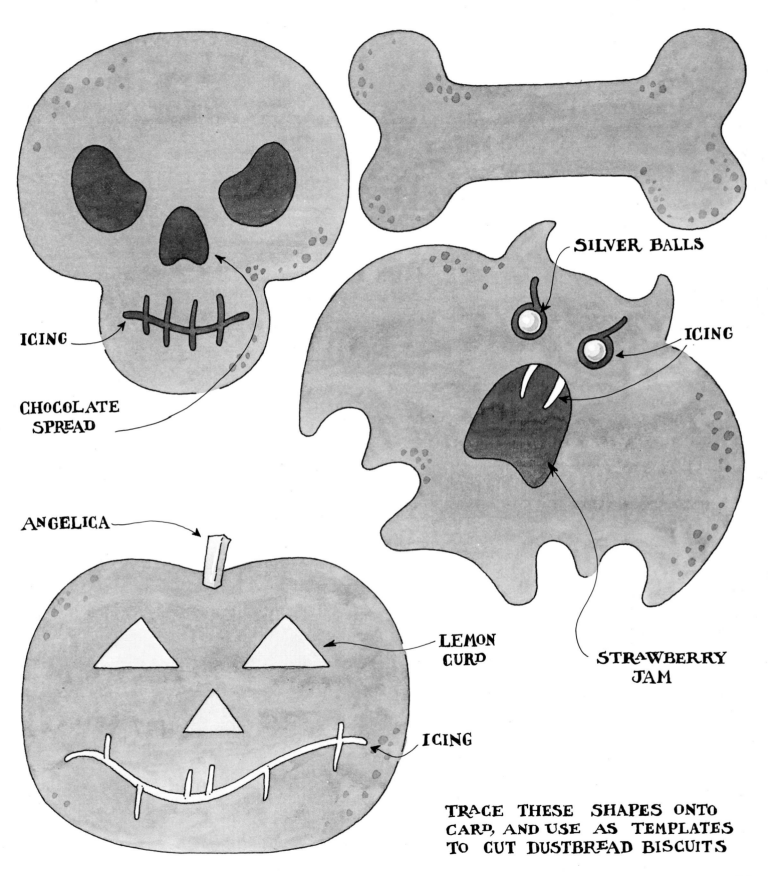

ICING

CHOCOLATE
SPREAD

SILVER BALLS

ICING

ANGELICA

LEMON
CURD

STRAWBERRY
JAM

ICING

TRACE THESE SHAPES ONTO
CARD, AND USE AS TEMPLATES
TO CUT DUSTBREAD BISCUITS

21

SORDID SAVOURIES

CHEESE BONES

INTO ½LB SHORTCRUST PASTRY, KNEAD 3oz GRATED HARD CHEESE, ½ TSP EACH OF DRY MUSTARD AND PAPRIKA...

...AND A PINCH OF SALT

← PASTRY

← HARD CHEESE

ROLL OUT TO ¼ INCH THICK AND CUT INTO STRIPS

SHAPE INTO BONES BY PINCHING WHERE SHOWN

PAPRIKA

BAKE AT 425°F* FOR ABOUT 13 MINUTES

ARRANGE PLEASINGLY

MUSTARD

*Gas mark 7

STAGNANT PONDS

MASH ONE AVOCADO WITH THE JUICE OF ONE LEMON, 1 TBS MAYONNAISE, AND SALT AND PEPPER TO TASTE

LEMON

← AVOCADO

← EGG

SPOON INTO PRE-COOKED TARTLET CASES

← MAYONNAISE

GARNISH WITH CHOPPED CRESS

← CRESS

TOMATO →

TOADSTOOLS

SLICE THE BOTTOM OFF A HARD-BOILED EGG. CUT A TOMATO IN HALF AND SCOOP OUT THE FLESH

PLACE TOMATO HALF ON THE EGG, SECURING WITH A DAB OF MAYONNAISE

DECORATE TOMATO WITH MAYONNAISE SPOTS

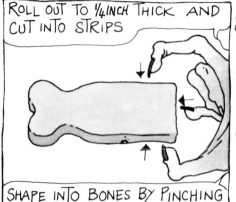

DUBIOUS TRIFLE

LINE A GLASS BOWL WITH SLICES OF STALE SPONGE CAKE

— SPONGE

MAKE FLIES FROM RAISINS AND FLAKED ALMONDS..

RAISIN →

CUT

← ALMOND

..AND TRAP THEM BETWEEN SPONGE AND BOWL

DRAIN SYRUP FROM A TIN OF FRUIT AND PLACE FRUIT OVER SPONGE

FRUIT →

MAKE A RED JELLY, POUR OVER FRUIT AND ALLOW TO SET.

JELLY →

MAKE A CHOCOLATE BLANCMANGE AND POUR OVER JELLY

← BLANCMANGE

WHEN THIS IS SET, PIPE CREAM TO FORM A SPIDER'S WEB

MAKE A SPIDER FROM A BLACK GRAPE WITH BOOTLACE LIQUORICE LEGS

GRAPE →

LIQUORICE →

MAKE MORE FLIES AND DECORATE TO TASTE

STRANGELY ENOUGH, THERE'S ALWAYS PLENTY OF THIS TRIFLE LEFT OVER!

WORM SOUP

RINSE ¼ LB LENTILS

←LENTILS

CHOP 2 ONIONS AND FRY GENTLY IN OIL WITH 2 CLOVES GARLIC

ONION
GARLIC→

ADD LENTILS, 3 PINTS COLD WATER, MIXED HERBS AND 1 TBS TOMATO PURÉE

HERBS

←TOMATO PURÉE

COOK COVERED FOR 30 MINUTES

TURNIP

SPAGHETTI

CARROTS→

ADD 2 CARROTS, SMALL TURNIP AND A PIECE OF CELERY — ALL CHOPPED FINELY

CELERY

COOK FOR 15 MINUTES

CHEESE

ADD SPAGHETTI BROKEN INTO WORM-SIZED PIECES AND COOK FOR A FURTHER 10 MINUTES

SEASON, AND SERVE GARNISHED WITH CHEESE

THIS IS NOT A MEAL TO BE EATEN OUTDOORS

POISON PIE

FRY ONE LARGE FINELY-CHOPPED ONION UNTIL SOFT AND ADD ½ LB SLICED FLAT MUSHROOMS. COOK FOR A FURTHER 5 MINUTES.

ADD 1 TBS FLOUR AND MIX. GRADUALLY ADD ¼ PINT MILK TO FORM A THICK SAUCE.

TAKE OFF HEAT AND ADD ONE BEATEN EGG, AND ONE DICED HARD-BOILED EGG.

MUSHROOM ← ONION   FLOUR   MILK → EGG

SEASON WITH SALT, PEPPER AND DILL

LINE PIE DISH WITH PUFF PASTRY AND POUR IN MIXTURE

TOP WITH PUFF PASTRY LID AND BRUSH WITH BEATEN EGG.

← DILL   SALT   ← PEPPER   EGG →

CUT SKULL AND CROSSBONES FROM SCRAPS OF PASTRY AND ARRANGE ON LID. BRUSH WITH BEATEN EGG.

BAKE AT 425°F* FOR 30 MINUTES.

* Gas mark 7

IT'S MORE FUN USING POISONOUS TOADSTOOLS BUT THEN YOU CAN ONLY EAT IT ONCE

CHAPTER 3
THE WITCH'S GARDEN

USEFUL HERBS

KNITBONE

A LEAF WILL DRAW OUT A SPLINTER OF WOOD FROM THE SKIN AND A POULTICE MADE FROM THE ROOT WILL SET BROKEN BONES AND EASE PAINFUL JOINTS.

MUGWORT

ONE LEAF PLACED IN THE SHOE ALLOWS THE WEARER TO TRAVEL GREAT DISTANCES WITHOUT FEELING TIRED—AND AN EGGCUPFUL OF JUICE LIFTS THE TIRED TRAVELLER.

SOAPWORT

THE BRUISED AND BOILED LEAVES MAKE A LATHERY LIQUID FOR WASHING CLOTHES AND WHEN APPLIED TO THE SKIN THIS LIQUID WILL ALSO CURE AN ITCH.

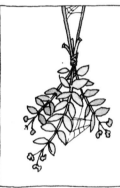

MYRTLE

WHEN GROWN INDOORS THIS PLANT BRINGS GOOD LUCK TO THE HOUSEHOLD. AN INFUSION MADE FROM THE LEAVES WILL MAKE A WITCH MORE BEAUTIFUL.

SAGE

THIS PLANT GROWS BEST FOR THE WISE. A CONSERVE MADE FROM THE FLOWERS HELPS AN AILING MEMORY. RUB A LEAF ON THE TEETH TO WHITEN THEM.

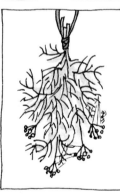

FENNEL

A BROTH MADE FROM THE ROOTS WILL BRING COLOUR BACK TO THE CHEEKS AFTER ILLNESS, AND WILL ALSO HELP FAT WITCHES TO BECOME THINNER.

HERBY GRASS

IT IS AN ANTIDOTE TO DEADLY POISON, BUT ONLY WHEN TAKEN BEFORE NOON. TO PROTECT SAGE FROM TOADS, PLANT HERBY GRASS ALL AROUND IT.

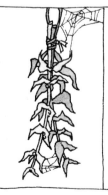

BALM

THE LEAVES STEEPED IN WINE ARE A REMEDY AGAINST THE BITE OF A MAD DOG. A SYRUP MADE FROM THE LEAVES SOOTHES ACHING TEETH.

GARDENING HINTS

MOSS AND SLIME WILL GROW ON STEPS THAT HAVE BEEN PAINTED WITH MILK.

TO ATTRACT SLUGS _ GROW ZINNIAS, ICELAND POPPIES, AND SPURGE. THEY ESPECIALLY LIKE THE YOUNG SHOOTS.

GROW ROSES TO ATTRACT GREENFLY, CABBAGE TO ATTRACT WHITEFLY, AND DAHLIAS FOR EARWIGS.

TO KILL A NEIGHBOUR'S STRAWBERRIES PLANT GLADIOLI NEARBY.

LEAVE FRUIT ON THE TREE TO ROT AND THERE WILL ALWAYS BE PLENTY OF WASPS IN THE GARDEN.

YELLOW IS THE FAVOURITE COLOUR OF INSECTS AND SO IF YOU WEAR IT THEY WILL ALWAYS SURROUND YOU.

29

THE PERFECT GARDEN

A WITCH NEEDN'T WAIT FOR HER PLANTS TO GROW, FOR SHE CAN TAKE THE BOREDOM OUT OF GARDENING WITH A WAVE OF HER WAND AND A MUTTERED SPELL — AND THIS WILL GIVE HER MORE TIME TO ENJOY A GARDEN LIKE THIS...

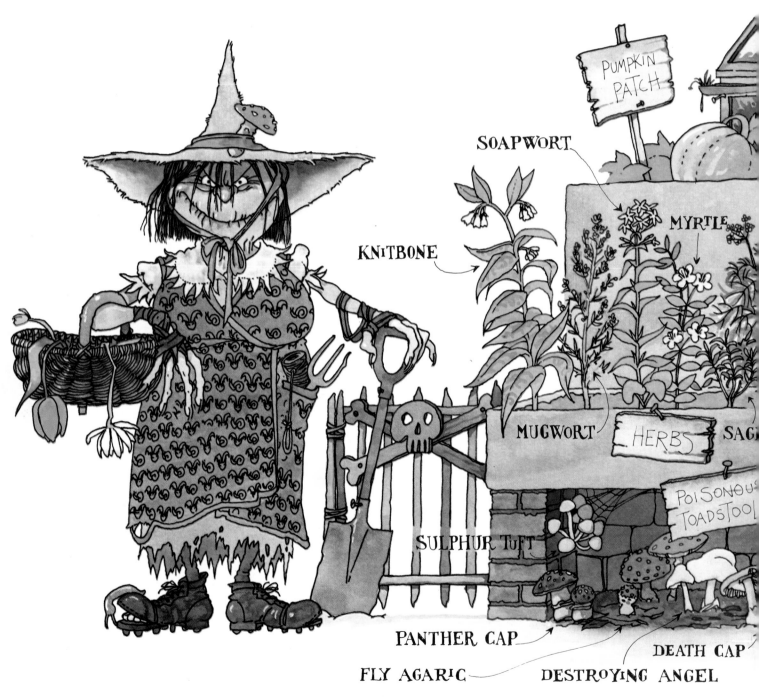

PUMPKIN PATCH

SOAPWORT

KNITBONE

MYRTLE

MUGWORT

HERBS

SAGE

SULPHUR TUFT

POISONOUS TOADSTOOL

PANTHER CAP

FLY AGARIC

DESTROYING ANGEL

DEATH CAP

DEADLY NIGHTSHADE

CUCKOO PINT

HENBANE

MONKSHOOD

FOXGLOVE

WHITE BRYONY

TOBACCO PLANT

STINKING IRIS

FENNEL

BALM

LUNGWORT

POISON PATCH
WASH YOUR HANDS
WHEN LEAVING

HATTIE'S PINCUSHION

ARUM LILY

FLOWERS

BLEEDING HEART

PONDLIFE

BOGBEAN

SLIME

BLANKET WEED

POND

SKUNK CABBAGE

DEW COLLECTOR

MIND YOUR OWN BUSINESS

WILDLIFE

MOUSE PLANT

31

UnSuiTABLe PLANTS

PLANTS GROWN FOR THEIR PLEASANT PERFUME, BRIGHT COLOUR OR ATTRACTION FOR BUTTERFLIES ARE QUITE UNSUITABLE FOR A WITCH'S GARDEN AND SHOULD BE AVOIDED AT ALL COSTS.

HOLLYHOCK

SUNFLOWER

BUDDLEIA

HYACINTH

DAFFODIL

STANDARD ROSE

PELARGONIUM

LILY OF THE VALLEY

GARDEN PESTS

PEST

REMEDY

NEIGHBOURS' CATS

GNOMES

FAIRIES

LADYBIRDS

LADYBIRD, LADYBIRD,
FLY AWAY HOME.
YOUR HOUSE IS ON FIRE
YOUR CHILDREN ARE GONE!

HOUSEHOLD PETS

Witches are not very happy sharing their homes with each other, so that if they need company (or help with the chores) they keep pets.

Any animal that lives with a witch is known as a familiar, though judging from their behaviour, one would hardly say they are friendly, especially to their owners.

Witches are very mean and begrudge feeding their pets, so the animals have to forage for food in nearby houses. This probably helps the belief that witches can assume animal form and so discover all that is going on. This rumour was, in fact, started by the witches themselves to imply that their magic powers were very great and also to frighten people. The spells that make it possible to change shape so drastically are known to only a few very old witches.

The cat is the most popular pet for a witch but this is not through any kindness on the witch's part, but simply because the cat is self sufficient and can usually look after itself. The pets shown here have all been seen living in a witch's home.

CAT
A WITCH SHOULD ALWAYS OWN A CAT, BUT THEY DO HAVE TO BE FED OFTEN — AND ON TIME.

GOAT
ALTHOUGH A STUBBORN ANIMAL, IT IS USEFUL FOR DESTROYING A NEIGHBOUR'S GARDEN.

SLUG
A QUIET LITTLE FRIEND TO HAVE BUT IT MUST BE KEPT AWAY FROM TREASURED PLANTS.

34

MAGPIE
NOT A PLEASANT BIRD BUT USEFUL IN ACQUIRING TRASHY JEWELLERY. CARE MUST BE TAKEN IN COLLECTING THIS.

SPIDER
NO TROUBLE TO KEEP AS THEY FIND THEIR OWN FOOD, AND ALSO PROVIDE MANY HOURS OF ENTERTAINMENT.

FROG
NEVER KISS A FROG OR IT MAY TURN INTO A PRINCE. FROGS ARE CHEAPER TO KEEP AND TAKE UP LESS ROOM.

BAT
UNLESS YOU KEEP LATE HOURS, THIS IS NOT A PET TO HAVE AS THEY'RE ALWAYS READY TO PLAY GAMES.

CHAPTER 4
FORTUNE-TELLING AND THE ZODIAC

THE WITCH'S ZODIAC

CAPRICORN
DECEMBER 23 TO JANUARY 20
SHREWD, CALCULATING AND VINDICTIVE. UNMOVED BY FLATTERY.

AQUARIUS
JANUARY 21 TO FEBRUARY 19
SLOW-GOING, DULL AND DISHONEST. HATES RESPONSIBILITY.

PISCES
FEBRUARY 20 TO MARCH 20
TIMID, WITH NO CONFIDENCE OR WILL-POWER. HAS A PERMANENT INFERIORITY COMPLEX.

CANCER
JUNE 22 TO JULY 22
GREEDY, SELFISH AND TOUCHY. WILL NOT ALLOW OTHERS TO MEDDLE.

LEO
JULY 23 TO AUGUST 22
TACTLESS, NARROW-MINDED, DOGMATIC AND RUTHLESS. LOVES GLITTER.

VIRGO
AUGUST 23 TO SEPTEMBER 22
CRUEL, CUNNING, NOSEY AND SNOBBISH. CANNOT BE MOVED TO PITY.

ARIES
MARCH 21 TO APRIL 20
IMPATIENT, SCHEMING
AND RASH. WILL NOT ADMIT
WHEN IN THE WRONG.

TAURUS
APRIL 21 TO MAY 22
FURIOUS TEMPER WHEN
FINALLY ROUSED. REVOLTED BY
UGLINESS IN OTHERS.

GEMINI
MAY 23 TO JUNE 21
RESTLESS, UNDEPENDABLE.
KIND-HEARTED WHEN
IT SUITS.

LIBRA
SEPTEMBER 23 TO OCTOBER 22
EASILY IMPRESSED AND
SLIGHTED. ALWAYS LOOKS
FOR THE EASY WAY OUT.

SCORPIO
OCTOBER 23 TO NOVEMBER 21
AMBITIOUS, SARCASTIC AND
VAIN. LOOKS ON OTHERS AS
PAWNS TO BE SACRIFICED.

SAGITTARIUS
NOVEMBER 22 TO DECEMBER 22
PATRONISING, SMUG
AND IMPULSIVE.
EXTREMELY OUTSPOKEN.

WITCHES' BIRTHDAYS

MONDAY'S WITCH IS FOUL OF FACE
TUESDAY'S WITCH IS A DISGRACE
WEDNESDAY'S WITCH IS LONG OF NOSE
THURSDAY'S WITCH HAS EXTRA TOES
FRIDAY'S WITCH BAKES POISONED PIES
SATURDAY'S WITCH HAS EVIL EYES
BUT THE WITCH THAT WAS BORN
ON THE SABBATH DAY
TENDS TO SMELL...
SO KEEP AWAY!

TEACUP READING

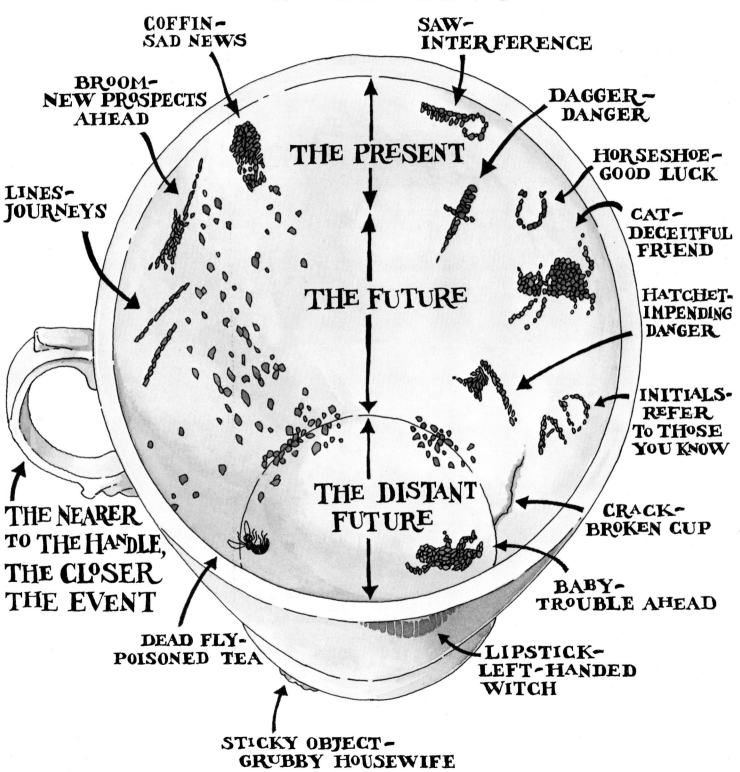

COFFIN - SAD NEWS

SAW - INTERFERENCE

DAGGER - DANGER

BROOM - NEW PROSPECTS AHEAD

HORSESHOE - GOOD LUCK

THE PRESENT

CAT - DECEITFUL FRIEND

LINES - JOURNEYS

THE FUTURE

HATCHET - IMPENDING DANGER

INITIALS - REFER TO THOSE YOU KNOW

THE DISTANT FUTURE

CRACK - BROKEN CUP

THE NEARER TO THE HANDLE, THE CLOSER THE EVENT

BABY - TROUBLE AHEAD

DEAD FLY - POISONED TEA

LIPSTICK - LEFT-HANDED WITCH

STICKY OBJECT - GRUBBY HOUSEWIFE

CHAPTER 5
CASTiNG SPELLS

EQUIPMENT

WINDFALL APPLES

BALE OF SPIDER WEBS

MAGIC DUST

VARIOUS HERBS

USED THINGS

BRIMSTONE

CHICORY LEAVES

SCREECH OWL'S FEATHERS

FAIRY'S TEARS

ASSORTED TEETH

DRAGON'S BLOOD

DRIED ADDER

EAGLE STONES

MANDRAKE

SAD STORIES

SABDEN PARKIN CRUMBS

FENNEL LEAF DEW

MORTAR AND PESTLE—FOR CRUSHING THINGS

ASH TWIG WAND

DEAD STOCKS WATER

BLACK PENNIES

CAULDRON

RED STRING

KNOT

44

THE MAGIC ORACLE

SPELLCASTING IS VERY COMPLICATED AND SOME WITCHES MAY NEED ADVICE. TO CONSULT THE ORACLE, CLOSE YOUR EYES AND, BY USING A PIN, CHOOSE A SQUARE. WRITE DOWN THIS AND EVERY EIGHTH LETTER. WHEN THE BOTTOM ROW IS REACHED, CONTINUE COUNTING ON THE FIRST ROW UNTIL THE FIRST LETTER NOTED IS REACHED. STARTING AT THE FIRST LETTER USED IN THE TOP ROW, READ OUT THE ADVICE.

45

GOOD LUCK CHARMS

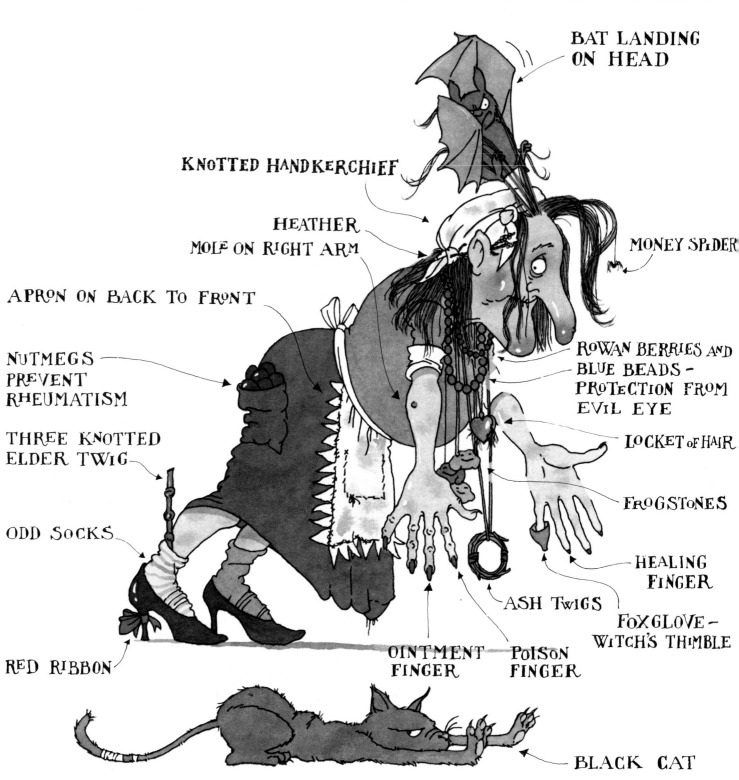

BAT LANDING ON HEAD

KNOTTED HANDKERCHIEF

HEATHER

MOLE ON RIGHT ARM

MONEY SPIDER

APRON ON BACK TO FRONT

NUTMEGS PREVENT RHEUMATISM

ROWAN BERRIES AND BLUE BEADS - PROTECTION FROM EVIL EYE

LOCKET OF HAIR

THREE KNOTTED ELDER TWIG

FROGSTONES

ODD SOCKS

HEALING FINGER

ASH TWIGS

FOXGLOVE - WITCH'S THIMBLE

RED RIBBON

OINTMENT FINGER

POISON FINGER

BLACK CAT

WITCHES BEWARE!

STRANGE AS IT MAY SEEM, SOME PEOPLE DO NOT LIKE WITCHES AND TAKE PRECAUTIONS TO STOP THEM FROM CROSSING THE THRESHOLD. LOOK OUT FOR THE FOLLOWING BEFORE ATTEMPTING TO ENTER.

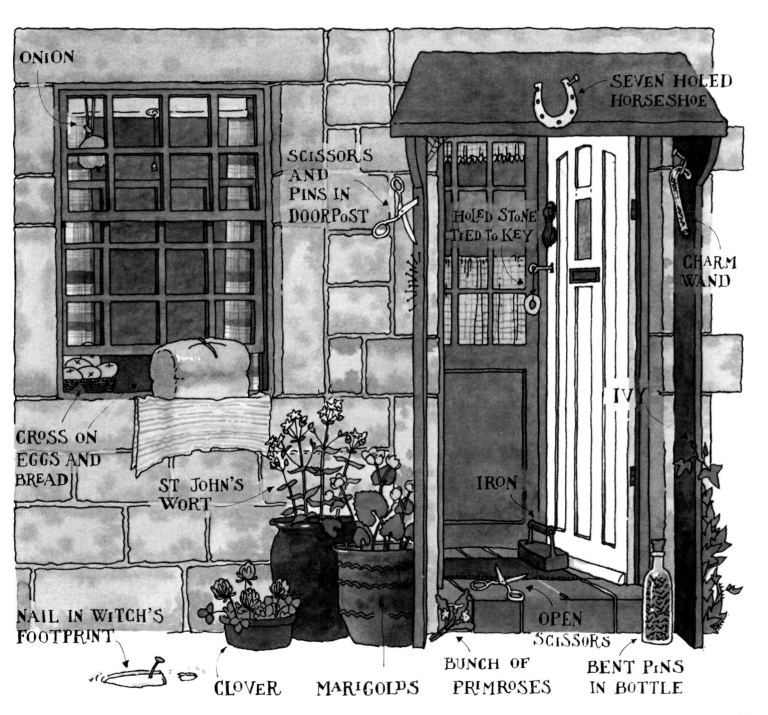

ONION

SEVEN HOLED HORSESHOE

SCISSORS AND PINS IN DOORPOST

HOLED STONE TIED TO KEY

CHARM WAND

IVY

CROSS ON EGGS AND BREAD

ST JOHN'S WORT

IRON

NAIL IN WITCH'S FOOTPRINT

CLOVER

MARIGOLDS

BUNCH OF PRIMROSES

OPEN SCISSORS

BENT PINS IN BOTTLE

SPELLS

Magic spells have been handed down through the years from witch to witch and old spell books are much sought after. Each spell usually consists of a verse that is chanted, while certain ingredients are stirred in a cauldron and the resulting fragrance (or nasty smell) sets the magic. Most verses clearly explain the spell but some, like the rain making one, have altered over the years of reciting so that they no longer make sense.

The witches here are shown in silhouette, partly because witches are not very good at writing rhymes and so feel foolish speaking them, but mainly so that if a spell does not work, then the identity of the witch demonstrating it remains a secret and she cannot be blamed. The spells have been simplified due to the unpleasant ingredients in some of them that were either difficult to find, very expensive to purchase, or were liable to deteriorate through storage (and usually because of all three reasons). Such ingredients have been omitted or replaced whilst still keeping the essence of the magic in each spell.

TO MAKE IT RAIN

RED WELLIES, YELLOW WELLIES
MIX THE HERBS WELL
WITH THE SMELLIES.
RED WELLIES, YELLOW WELLIES-
MAKE IT RAIN!

MIX ONE CUP OF FAIRY TEARS WITH ONE RAINCOAT BUTTON AND STIR WITH AN UMBRELLA HANDLE. POUR INTO WELLINGTONS, PLACE ON FEET, AND CHANT SPELL.

TO CURE MAD CATTLE

THE BLACK PENNY DIPPED IN SOUTH RUNNING STREAM CURES MADNESS IN CATTLE AND CURDLING IN CREAM.

FIND A BLACK PENNY AT THE FOOT OF A SPINDLE TREE. TIE TO A WITCH'S HAIR, AND DIP IN THE STREAM. COMPARED WITH THIS BEHAVIOUR, THE CATTLE WILL APPEAR SANE.

TO REGAIN THE MEMORY

TAKE SIX LEAVES OF PALSYWORT MAKE A STEAMING BREW TO CLEAR LOSS OF MEMORY AND VERTIGO TOO.

COLLECT SIX YOUNG LEAVES OF PALSYWORT AND STEAM UNTIL TENDER. ALLOW TO COOL THEN BIND TO FOREHEAD. WHEN ASKED, YOU WILL REMEMBER WHY YOU DID THIS.

TO STRENGTHEN SIGHT

FOUND NEAR TO THE CROSSROADS CLOSE TO MIDNIGHT DEW FROM THE FENNEL LEAF STRENGTHENS THE SIGHT.

COLLECT ONE TEACUPFUL OF DEW FROM FENNEL LEAVES, STEEP A FRESH SPIDER'S WEB IN IT FOR SEVEN HOURS. USE TO CLEAN SPECTACLE LENSES.

TO BECOME INVISIBLE

IF INVISIBLE YOU WOULD BE TAKE THREE LEAVES OF CHICORY. TO UNLOCK A BOX OR DOOR USE THE STRENGTH OF TWENTY FOUR.

MIX CHICORY LEAVES WITH WATER FROM VASE OF DEAD STOCKS. SOAK A PURPLE CLOAK IN IT UNTIL SMELLY, THEN WEAR IT. PEOPLE WILL NOT BE ABLE TO SEE YOU.

TO SUMMON THE WIND

EACH KNOT I MAKE AND THEN UNTIE WILL STIR THE WIND TO FILL THE SKY.

TIE SEVERAL KNOTS IN A PIECE OF RED STRING THAT IS AS LONG AS YOUR SHADOW. AS EACH KNOT IS UNDONE, THE WIND WILL BLOW STRONGER.

TO ENCOURAGE VISITORS

PRICK WITH TWELVE PINS AN APPLE ALL GREEN SHRIEK THE NAME OF THE GUEST TO BE SEEN.

INTO A GREEN WINDFALL APPLE, THRUST TWELVE PINS, AND SCREAM OUT A PERSON'S NAME. WITHIN MINUTES, YOU WILL HEAR A KNOCK AT THE DOOR.

CHAPTER 6
OLD WIVES' TALES

THE TALES

THESE ARE SOME OLD WIVES' TALES THAT ALL WITCHES NEED TO KNOW. BEWARE OF THE TRUTHS CONTAINED IN THEM.

If a woman should desire to marry within the year then she should gather St John's Wort early in the morning of St Agnes's Eve (20th January) whilst the dew is still on the plant.

Clothes fret for their owner, so that a person's health can be seen from the condition of the clothes they have left behind.

If cowslips (also known as palsywort) are planted upside down the flowers will be red and not yellow.

A garter made from an eelskin will prevent cramp, and a live eel placed in a drink will cure those who drink too much.

A remedy for nosebleeds is to stick the leaves of the nettle up the nostrils.

Ivy leaves soaked in vinegar and bound to corns will cure them.

The appearance of a white cricket on the hearth spells doom.

The only way for a mandrake to be picked safely is to loosen the earth around it with an ivory or iron pick, then tie a dog to it. Tempt the dog with meat and the mandrake will be pulled out. All who hear the shriek of a mandrake will die so your ears must be covered and these precautions always taken.

It is unlucky to sit under a hawthorn tree on May Day, Midsummer Eve or Halloween as the fairies will carry you away. It is, however, a strong protection from lightning if a sprig of hawthorn is kept in the house.

To make a rainbow disappear, make a cross of sticks with a stone at the end of each stick.

If a plate of flour is placed under a rosemary bush on Midsummer Eve, your future husband's initials will be found there next morning.

Rosemary tea aids failing memory.

A Stamp Stainer is a person who can heal an affected part of the body by stamping on it.

Pigs running about with straws in their mouth foretell the coming of windy weather.

Bees hate quarrels and swearing and will leave the hive if they should hear any.

To cure warts, rub a pod containing nine peas on them and they will dry away. Another remedy is to touch each wart with a different pea on the first day of the new moon, wrap the peas in a cloth and throw them away over the shoulder. Whoever picks up the cloth will get your warts.

Teeth that fall out should always be sprinkled with salt and burnt rather than be thrown away as a witch might find them and use them in a spell against their owner.

If a four-leaved clover is worn in the right shoe, then the first man met on the journey will be the future husband.

Orpine (also called livelong) should be hung in the house as a repellent for flies and disease.

It is unlucky to step over a crawling child as it will stunt its growth.

A Blackberry Cat is one born near to Michaelmas and will always be full of mischief.

To cure cramp one must wear a garter of corks round the leg.

To hear fairies laughing near a fairy ring you must run nine times round the ring clockwise – to run the other way is to put yourself in their power.

Earrings are good for the sight if bought with money collected from a member of the opposite sex, who hasn't been thanked for the gift. This only applies to earrings for pierced ears.

The number of croaks given by the first crow seen in the morning foretells the day's weather – an even number means good weather, and an odd number means storms. The chattering of crows spells misfortune and persistent croaking denotes rain. If one crow flies over a house it means a birth, two mean a wedding, and three bring good luck.

To cure a wound always apply grease to the thing that caused it.

It is unlucky to turn the mattress on a bed on Sunday, Friday or Monday (and especially so if someone is still in the bed).

An itching corn means that rain will fall within hours.

If a garment is accidentally put on inside out it should be left that way, but if the buttons are done up wrongly the garment must be taken off and put on again so as to avert the evil eye.

A bay tree grown near the house will protect it from plague and lightning. A bay leaf placed under the pillow will induce sweet dreams.

If a bay leaf thrown onto the fire burns noisily, it means good luck; if it burns silently with lots of smoke it means bad luck.

Lighting three candles in a room is unlucky – those that do, will quarrel. If there is a spark in the wick of a lit candle it means the arrival of a letter for the person nearest the candle. The candle should be knocked until the spark drops off, the number of knocks indicates the number of days before the letter will arrive.

A circlet of ash leaves worn on the head is a protection from adders.

The houseleek (also called syngreen) when grown on the roof of a house will protect it from fire.

If someone is struck by lightning they should be buried up to their neck in earth to heal them.

CHAPTER 7
STAYING BEAUTIFUL

ANYONE CAN LOOK

LIKE A WITCH

BEAUTY SECRETS

WATER IN WHICH EGGS HAVE BEEN BOILED IS SPLENDID FOR CAUSING WARTS. SIMPLY SOAK THE FACE AND HANDS IN IT FOR SEVERAL DAYS.

IN AN EMERGENCY, SPIDERS CAN BE USED AS FALSE EYELASHES, BUT IT IS WISE TO KEEP SPARES IN CASE THEY WANDER OFF.

IF YOU'RE UNHAPPY WITH THE WAY YOU LOOK, MAKE A FACE MASK OF HONEY, GARLIC AND ONION, AND LEAVE IT ON. YOU'LL BE SURPRISED AT THE IMPROVEMENT.

TO ECONOMIZE ON EYESHADOW, TRY NOT TO SLEEP FOR SEVERAL NIGHTS. YOUR EYES WILL SOON BE SURROUNDED BY VERY DARK RINGS.

BILBERRIES CAN BE USED AS A LIPSTICK, ALTHOUGH IT IS DIFFICULT TO BE ACCURATE, AND ONCE APPLIED THE STAIN IS IMPOSSIBLE TO REMOVE.

IF HAIR IS IN VERY GOOD CONDITION, IT SHOULD BE PERMED AND THEN BLEACHED. THIS WILL COARSEN IT AND SPLIT MOST OF THE ENDS.

RATHER THAN RESORT TO PLASTIC SURGERY TO LIFT YOUR FEATURES, TRY TYING YOUR HAIR VERY TIGHTLY INTO A BUN. THE YEARS WILL SLIP AWAY.

IF YOUR SKIN LOOKS TOO PURE, A HEAVY DIET OF CHOCOLATE AND SWEETS WILL RECTIFY THIS CONDITION AND CAUSE HEAVY SPOTTING.

CHAPTER 8
THE FASHIONABLE WITCH

RECYCLING OLD CLOTHES

CHILD'S SCARF
WORN AS TURBAN

ROADWORK CONE
WITH COVERING
REMOVED

OLD SHIRTS
WORN FOR A
LAYERED LOOK

SCHOOL TIE
SLEEVE
BINDINGS

REFUSE SACK
SPLIT OPEN AND
TUCKED INTO SKIRT

TEA STAINED
TABLECLOTH
GATHERED
ONTO ROPE

STICKING PLASTER
DECORATION

ODD SOCKS CUT
UP AND USED AS
LEGWARMERS

TEARS
COVERED WITH
PATCHES

DIRTY
BLANKET
USED AS
CLOAK

FASHION HINTS

BRIGHTEN UP AN OLD BLOUSE WITH WORM EMBROIDERY - BRIBE THEM TO KEEP STILL.

IF THERE IS ANY PROBLEM ACCESSORISING AN OUTFIT, DYE EVERYTHING IN YOUR WARDROBE BLACK.

TO MAKE SURE THAT A SKIRT HEM IS CROOKED, WEAR ODD SHOES WHEN MEASURING IT.

TO OBTAIN A UNIQUE PATTERNED DRESS, COVER THE TABLE AT A MESSY PARTY WITH YOUR PLAIN FROCK

FOR A LACE DRESS THAT COSTS NEXT TO NOTHING, TRAIN SPIDERS TO CROCHET.

TO MAKE SURE THAT YOUR BEST FROCK GETS STAINED, DO THE WASHING UP JUST BEFORE GOING OUT.

KNITTING PATTERNS

Witches are very loath to part with money and so the idea of something for nothing is very appealing to them. Most of them can knit after a fashion and so these four knitting patterns will be of immense use – each item can be made over and over again in a variety of colours to provide those little accessories that can revamp a whole wardrobe.

Amounts of yarn given are only an approximate guide as yarn from different manufacturers varies considerably, although the miserly witch will be able to obtain wool by unravelling old sweaters, tying the wool in skeins and washing thoroughly.

It may be a chore but the tension square must be knitted or the finished result will have no chance of coming out to the correct measurements.

ABBREVIATIONS

K = knit; P = purl; sts = stitches; st-st = stocking stitch (one row knit, one row purl); g-st = garter stitch (every row knit); comm = commencing; cont = continue; rem = remaining; tog = together; inc = increase by working into front and back of next stitch; dec = decrease by working 2 stitches together; beg = beginning; SL1= slip one stitch knitwise; PSSO pass slipped stitch over; alt alternate.

BOBBLE HAT

YARN: 2 x 50gm balls of double knitting in black, and 1 ball in cream.
NEEDLES: 1 pair of 4mm (No. 8).
TENSION: 22 sts and 28 rows to 10cm (4in) square.

HAT:
With 4mm needles and black cast on 114 sts and cont in st-st comm with a K row.
Work 12 rows.
Work bones thus: Row 1: Reading from right to left knit first

row of graph 6 times, working light sts in cream.
Row 2: Reading from left to right purl second row of graph 6 times.

Cont in this manner until all 17 rows of the graph have been worked.
Cont in st-st with black, and comm with a P row work 4 rows.
Next row: K.
Cont in st-st comm with a K row and work 58 rows.

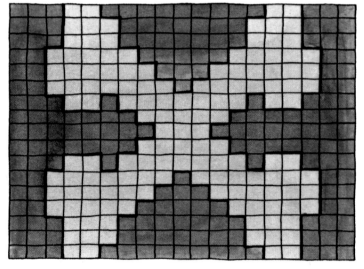

Shape crown: Row 1: (Sl 1, K1, PSSO, K15, K2 tog) to end.
Row 2 and every alt row: P.
Row 3: (SL 1, K1, PSSO, K13, K2 tog) to end.

Cont in this manner, decreasing number of K sts by 2 each time until following row has been worked:
(Sl1, K1, PSSO, K1, K2 tog) to end.
Next row: P.
Next row: (Sl1, K2 tog, PSSO) to end.
Break yarn and thread through sts on needle, drawing up tightly.

TO MAKE UP:
Join seam. Fold back hem and sew down. Make 1 skull bobble and sew to top of hat.

BOBBLE

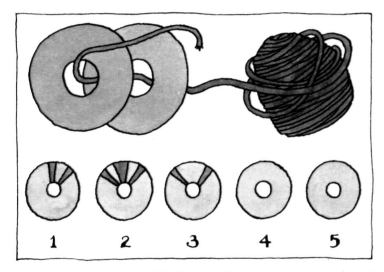

TO MAKE BOBBLES: Cut two 10cm (4in) circles of card with a 2.5cm (1in) hole in the centre. Place rings together and, using cream and black wool, wind yarn over cards as shown, covering completely five times following diagrams 1-5. Push scissor points through wool at outside edge and between the two layers of card and cut all round.
Take a length of yarn, slide between the two layers of card and tie round tightly.
Slide off card rings and trim bobble with scissors to form skull shape.
Attach to scarf and hat using remainder of tying yarn.

BOBBLE SCARF

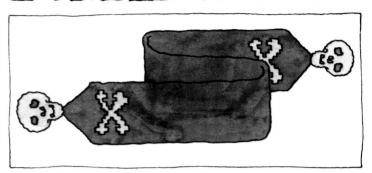

YARN: 4 x 50gm balls of double knitting in black, and 1 x 50gm ball in cream.
NEEDLES: 1 pair of 4mm (No. 8) and a stitch holder.
TENSION: 22 sts and 28 rows to 10cm (4in) square.

SCARF:
*With 4mm needles and black cast on 3 sts and cont in st-st comm with a K row.
Work 2 rows.
Inc 1 st at beg of next and every following row until there are 33 sts on the needle *.
Break yarn and push work to end of needle.
Work from * to * once more.
Cont in st-st, comm with a K row, and work across both sets of sts (66 sts).
Work 4 rows.
Work bones thus:
Row 1: (K7 black, reading from right to left knit first row of graph, working light stitches in cream, K7) twice.
Row 2: (P7 black, reading from left to right purl second row of graph, P7) twice.
Cont in this manner until all 17 rows of graph have been worked.
Cont in st-st with black, and comm with a P row work 319 rows, ending with a P row.
Work bones as before.
Cont in st-st with black, and comm with a P row work 5 rows.
Next row: K2 tog, K31, slip rem 33 sts on to a stitch holder.

Dec 1 st at beg of next and every following row until 3 sts remain.
Cast off.
Rejoin yarn to held sts and dec 1 st at beg of next and every following row until 3 sts remain.
Cast off.

TO MAKE UP:
Join seam and pointed ends. Make 2 skull bobbles and sew one to each end of scarf.

EVERYDAY HAT

YARN: Hat – 5 x 50gm balls of black chunky yarn.
Hatband – 1 x 50gm ball each of red and cream double knitting.
NEEDLES 1 pair each of 4mm (No. 8) and 6mm (No. 4).
PLUS: 1m 20cm of black covered millinery wire.
TENSION: 15 sts and 20 rows to 10cm square, measured over garter stitch on 6mm needles with chunky yarn.
22 sts and 34 rows to 10cm square, measured over garter stitch on 4mm needles with double knitting.

HAT:
With 6mm needles and chunky yarn cast on 77 sts and cont in g-st.
Work 16 rows.

Next row: (K2 tog, K9) to end.
Work 7 rows.
Next row: (K2 tog, K8) to end.
Work 7 rows.
Next row: (K2 tog, K7) to end.
Work 7 rows.
Next row: (K2 tog, K6) to end.
Work 7 rows.
Next row: (K2 tog, K5) to end.
Work 7 rows.
Next row: (K2 tog, K4) to end.
Work 7 rows.
Next row: (K2 tog, K3) to end.
Work 7 rows.
Next row: (K2 tog, K2) to end.
Work 7 rows.
Next row: (K2 tog, K1) to end.
Work 7 rows.
Next row: (K2 tog) to end.
Work 7 rows.
Next row: (K2 tog) 3 times, K1.
Work 7 rows.
Next row: (K2 tog) twice, slip first st over second, break yarn and draw through st.
Brim: Pick up and K77 sts from cast on edge of hat and cont in g-st.
Work 1 row.
Next row: (Inc 1, K6) to end.
Work 1 row.
Next row: (Inc 1, K7) to end.
Work 1 row.
Next row: (Inc 1, K8) to end.
Work 3 rows.
Next row: (Inc 1, K9) to end.
Work 3 rows.
Next row: (Inc 1, K4) to last st, K1.
Work 5 rows.
Cast off.

HATBAND:
With 4mm needles and cream double knitting cast on 18 sts

and cont in g-st thus:

Rows 1, 3, 6 and 8: (K3 cream, K3 red) three times.
Rows 2, 4, 5 and 7: (K3 red, K3 cream) three times.
Cont working check pattern, keeping strands to back of work, until band measures 60 cms.
Cast off.

TO MAKE UP:

Sew hat seam. Blanket stitch wire to edge of brim with black yarn, overlapping ends by 2cm. Join short ends of hatband and catch in place with a few stitches.

USEFUL MITTENS

YARN: 1 x 50gm ball of black double knitting; a small amount of silver lurex 4 ply.
NEEDLES: 1 pair each of 4mm (No. 8) and 3¼4mm (No. 10), 2 stitch holders and a safety pin.
TENSION: 22sts and 28 rows to 10cm square, measured over st-st.

LEFT HAND:

With 3¼4mm needles cast on 41 sts and work 30 rows K1, P1 rib.
Change to 4mm needles.
Cont in st-st, comm with a K row, and work 20 rows.

DIVIDE FOR THUMB:

K34, slip the rem 7sts on to a safety pin, then cast on 7 sts.
Comm with a P row, work 15 rows st-st.
** Break yarn, and slip first 15 sts onto a stitch holder, With 3¼4mm needles work 1 row K1, P1 rib on the next 11 sts.
Slip the rem 15 sts onto a stitch holder.
Working on the 11 sts, work 5 more rows K1, P1 rib.

Cast off loosely in rib.
Sew up rib seam to form finger hole.

NEXT FINGER:

Pick up 5sts from one stitch holder, 3sts from base of finger rib already worked, and 5sts from other stitch holder (13 sts).
Work 6 rows K1, P1 rib.
Cast off loosely in rib and join seam.
Repeat this last process twice.

THUMB RIB:

With 3¼4mm needles pick up the 7 cast on sts, 3sts from gap between cast on sts and those on safety pin, and 7 sts from safety pin (17 sts).
Work 6 rows K1, P1 rib.
Cast off loosely in rib and join seam.

RIGHT HAND:

With 3¼4mm needles cast on 41sts and work 30 rows K1, P1 rib.
Change to 4mm needles.
Cont in st-st, comm with a K row, and work 19 rows.

DIVIDE FOR THUMB:

P34, slip the rem 7 sts on to a safety pin, then cast on 7 sts.
Comm with a K row, work 16 rows st-st.
Repeat as for left hand from ** to end.

MOON:

With 3¼4mm needles and lurex cast on 8sts and cont in g-st.
Work 1 row.
Inc 1st at beg of every row until there are 13sts on the needle.
Next row: Cast off 6sts, K to end.
Work 13 rows.
Next row: Cast on 6 sts, K to end.
Dec 1 st at beg of every row until 8sts rem.
Cast off.

Make a second moon.
Position on back of gloves and slip stitch in place. For extra sparkle sew on star-shaped sequins. Join glove seam.

CHAPTER 9
HOBBIES AND CRAFTS

CRAZY QUILT

MOST QUILTS ARE NOT FOR THE AMATEUR AND SO A LITTLE DIFFICULTY MAY HAVE BEEN ENCOUNTERED PREVIOUSLY.

THE CRAZY QUILT IS SIMPLE— IT NEEDS NO PATTERN AND A VERY RANDOM SELECTION OF FABRICS.

PLACE A SHEET ON THE FLOOR, THEN FLY INTO A RAGE. CUT UP ALL THE FABRIC IN PIECES AND HURL IT INTO THE AIR.

BEGIN IN ONE CORNER OF THE SHEET AND, HEMMING EACH EDGE AS YOU GO, OVERLAP ALL BITS OF FABRIC UNTIL THE QUILT IS DONE.

TEACOSIES
SKULL COSY

MATERIALS: 35cm x 90cm wide each of black felt and lining; 30cm square white felt; wadding; embroidery silk; matching thread. Enlarge the diagram below by making each square measure 3cm and trace off: 1) teacosy pattern; 2) skull and crossbone motif (out line only); 3) bottom edge facing (5cm wide).

Cut out two teacosy pieces each in black felt and lining; one motif in white felt (cutting the holes for eyes, nose and teeth); two facings in black felt. Position the motif on one of the teacosy pieces and, using embroidery silk, blanket stitch in place – outlining the skull and bones as shown.

Mount each teacosy piece onto wadding and, with both right sides of felt together, take a 1cm seam along the curved edge. Turn to the right side and, having seamed the two facings together, blanket stitch them along the bottom edge.

Join the lining and, taking a 3cm hem, hand stitch in place.

BAT COSY

MATERIALS: 35cm x 90cm each of black felt and lining; 12cm x 18cm red felt; wadding; embroidery silk; matching thread. Enlarge the diagram below by making each square measure 3cm and trace off: 1) teacosy pattern; 2) eye and mouth backing piece (to broken line); 3) bottom edge facing. Cut out two teacosy pieces in black felt and lining (cutting latter to 2cm below the horizontal broken line only). In one of the teacosy pieces cut out eye and mouth holes. Cut out the backing piece in red felt and, placing it behind the features, blanket stitch in place.

Mount each teacosy piece onto wadding, cutting back the wadding 5mm from the felt edge. With wadding sides together, blanket stitch round the edge, except at the bottom. Cut out two facings in black felt and, joining with a tiny seam, blanket stitch along the inside of the bottom edge. Taking a tiny seam join the lining and handstitch into place, taking a 1cm hem. Quilt along dotted lines.

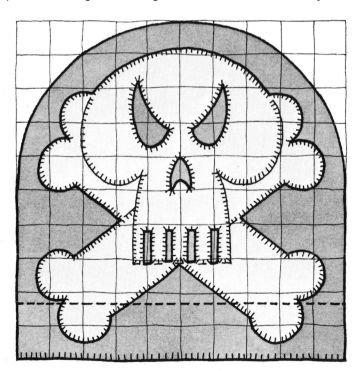

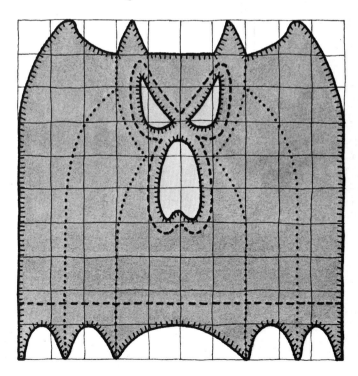

STENCILLING WALLS

A CHEAP WAY TO DECORATE A WALL IS TO STENCIL IT BY PAINTING ROUND OBJECTS WHICH HAVE BEEN ARRANGED IN A PLEASING DESIGN. PROTECTIVE CLOTHING MUST ALWAYS BE WORN, AS SOME OF THE OBJECTS MAY HAVE A TENDENCY TO STRUGGLE.

A USEFUL RUG

A rug can be most useful in disguising soiled floors, hiding a trap door to a secret tunnel, or for covering the burnt patches of carpet near to the fireplace. Rugmaking can fill many a wintry evening and several witches could work together to make a rug between them, though the arguments to establish the ownership of such a rug may make this an impractical idea. The rug shown here is a perfect size for any room.

measures 166cm x 83cm when finished, has 20,000 holes in it. This means that there are 20,000 little strands of wool to hook in. If it takes 1 minute to hook 5 strands, then it will take 67 hours to finish the rug. If you can work for 2 hours a day on this, it will take 34 days. Witches are not known for their patience and will get crabby and peevish (more so than usual). So you must decide before you put hook to canvas – do you need this rug? If you think that your home needs this luxury item then begin it in the autumn and by the spring time you will have finished it, but if you feel that you can manage without it then turn the page and make a cushion instead.

INSTRUCTIONS

MATERIALS: 180cm x 90cm wide rug canvas with 3 holes per 2.5cm; 66 packs of 68mm length rug wool with 320 pieces per pack (29 packs of blue, 11 purple, 11 black, 7 pink, 7 yellow, 1 red); rug hook.

Now, a word of warning before beginning this rug. Spend some time thinking what you are taking on. The rug, which

Here is the method though, should you need it. Transfer the design to canvas with an indelible crayon, leaving a 4 hole hem on all four sides. Fold hems to right side and, beginning at the bottom right hand corner, hook away horizontally in rows until the rug is complete, working through both layers on hems.

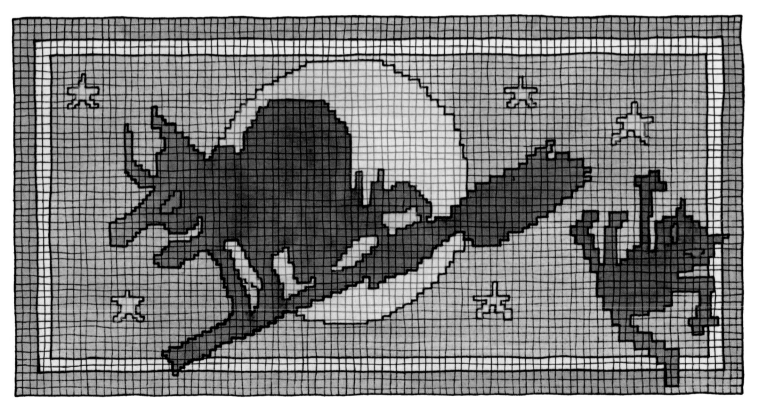

ONE SQUARE REPRESENTS FOUR HOLES ON THE CANVAS.

CUSHIONS

MATERIALS: For each cushion – scraps of fabric; 46cm square cushion pad or stuffing material; embroidery silk; matching thread; 40cm zip. Each cushion consists of a central 36cm square, a pieced border of four 6cm squares and four 6cm x 36cm rectangles, a motif which is appliqued to the assembled cushion front, and a plain 48cm square back. To obtain the pattern pieces enlarge each cushion design by making each square measure 6cm and trace off: 1) central square; 2) border square; 3) border rectangle; 4) cushion back – adding 7mm turnings on each edge. Trace 5) motif – adding a 5mm turning if it is to be sewn on with a hem folded underneath, or without turnings if it is to be backed with iron-on interlining and satin or blanket stitched on.

Cut out all cushion pieces and seam together the cushion front. Sew on the motif adding details with embroidery or appliqued fabric. With right sides of cushion together sew in the zip centered along one side and then seam the remaining edges. Turn to the right side and insert cushion pad. Close zip.

THE BROOMSTICK

A WITCH'S BROOMSTICK IS ONE OF HER MOST IMPORTANT PIECES OF EQUIPMENT. IT IS USEFUL IN THE HOME AND ALSO PROVIDES A CHEAP FORM OF TRANSPORT.

MAKING A BROOMSTICK

BIRCH, BROOM OR HEATHER

PUSH HANDLE INTO BROOMHEAD

BANG ONTO HARD SURFACE

SECURE WITH NAIL

FLYING

THE MODERN VERSION OF THE BROOMSTICK DOES HAVE ITS LIMITATIONS.

DO NOT ATTEMPT TOO MUCH ON THE FIRST TRIAL FLIGHT.

SHOULD A BROOMSTICK PROVE UNSUITABLE, IT CAN BE PUT TO MANY USES.

77

CHAPTER 10
FESTIVITIES

HALLOWEEN

WITCHES LOVE ANY EXCUSE TO HAVE FUN AND THROW A PARTY, AND HALLOWEEN IS THE MAIN FESTIVAL OF THE YEAR. HERE ARE SOME SIMPLE WAYS TO CELEBRATE THE 31ST OF OCTOBER.

DECORATIONS

GARLANDS—
SKULL & CROSSBONES

BATS

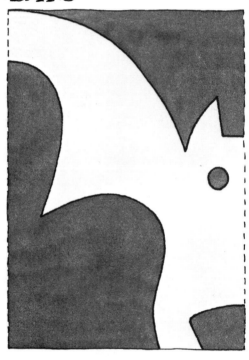

PAPER SOILIES

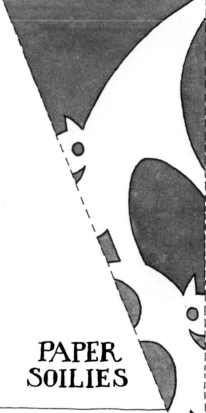

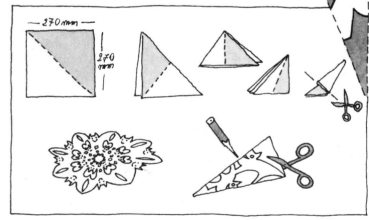

CARVING THE PUMPKIN

NIGHTLIGHT

A TYPICAL BANQUET

JUDITH'S PUMPKIN CHIFFON PIE

★ DUBIOUS TRIFLE

★ WORM SOUP

★ DUSTBREAD BISCUITS

TOADSTOOLS

★ STAGNANT PONDS

★ KNEEBONES

PECAN PIE

PUMPKIN SOUP

★ POISON PIE

UNWELCOME GUEST

★ SEE CHAPTER 2

HALLOWEEN FUN

TRICK OR TREAT

WITCHES VISIT NEIGHBOURHOOD HOUSES ASKING FOR TREATS. THE THREAT OF PLAYING A TRICK IS SELDOM NEEDED—ONE LOOK AT A WITCH'S FACE IS ENOUGH.

CRACK THE MIRROR

EACH WITCH MUST TRY TO CRACK AS MANY MIRRORS AS POSSIBLE BY STARING INTO THEM. THIS CAN BE A VERY EXPENSIVE GAME TO PLAY.

HUNT THE PUMPKIN

ONE WITCH GOES OUT OF THE ROOM, WHILST THE REMAINING WITCHES HIDE A PUMPKIN IN AN INCONSPICUOUS PLACE.

APPLE DUCKING

APPLES ARE FLOATED IN A CONTAINER OF WATER AND EACH WITCH MUST REMOVE THE APPLES WITHOUT USING HER HANDS.

PASS THE BAT

A BAT IS PASSED ROUND WHILE MUSIC PLAYS. EACH TIME IT STOPS THE WITCH HOLDING THE BAT DROPS OUT. THE LAST WITCH KEEPS THE BAT.

ODD ONE OUT

THE MOST UNPOPULAR WITCH LEAVES THE ROOM AND HIDES. THE OTHER WITCHES COUNT TO 113, THEN GO ON TO ANOTHER PARTY.

ROOM ON THE BROOM?

SEE HOW MANY WITCHES CAN CLIMB ON TO A HOVERING BROOMSTICK BEFORE IT FALLS TO THE GROUND.

SLUG-LA

EACH WITCH THROWS SLUGS OVER THE POINT OF A WITCH'S HAT TO WIN A BOWL OF PIRANHA FISH.

WITCHES WORLDWIDE

AMERICA

AUSTRALIA

BRITAIN

GERMANY

HOLLAND

ITALY

WITCHES IN OTHER LANDS CELEBRATE FESTIVALS IN THEIR OWN SPECIAL COSTUMES

CANADA

FINLAND

FRANCE

JAPAN

SPAIN

SWEDEN

CHRISTMAS

CHRISTMAS IS NOT A FESTIVAL THAT WITCHES ACTUALLY CELEBRATE, BUT THEY DERIVE MUCH PLEASURE FROM SPOILING IT FOR OTHER PEOPLE. IF A WITCH SEES SOMEONE ENJOYING CHRISTMAS, SHE FEELS IT IS HER DUTY TO INTERFERE.

SPOOKY GROTTO

WITCHES HAVE BEEN KNOWN TO TAKE OVER THE CHRISTMAS GROTTO IN A DEPARTMENT STORE JUST TO GIVE FATHER CHRISTMAS A BAD REPUTATION.

HUGGINS & WILMOTT WISH ALL THEIR CUSTOMERS A VERY MERRY CHRISTMAS

LUCKY DIP

THE REAL FATHER CHRISTMAS

PRESENTS REPLACED WITH BRICKS

GRUBBY CRACKERS

TRY THIS TO SPOIL A PARTY — USING A FUNNEL, FILL CHRISTMAS CRACKERS WITH SOOT, FLOUR OR HOUSEHOLD DUST.

HOLLY SURPRISE

DO NOT WASTE HOLLY BY HANGING IT ON THE WALL. PLACE SPRIGS OF IT IN UNEXPECTED PLACES.

VILE TREE TRIMS

FROG INSTEAD OF FAIRY

SLUG AND RIBBON CANES

WORMS AS TINSEL

FROGSPAWN BAUBLES

MOTHBALL GARLANDS

BRING A SHUDDER TO SOMEONE'S CHRISTMAS DAY BY REPLACING REGULAR TREE DECORATIONS WITH THE ABOVE.

FESTIVE FOOD

SKATING ACCIDENT CAKE

FRUIT CAKE + CAKE DECORATIONS + WHITE AND BLACK ICING =

AVALANCHE TRIFLE

CREAM
FRUIT & JELLY
SPONGE

TRIFLE + CAKE DECORATION + MERINGUE =

YULE BROOMSTICK

SWISS ROLL + MARZIPAN + BUTTER CREAM =

SPOONBENDER PUDDING

IRON + PUDDING MIXTURE + HOLLY =

CHRISTMAS FUN

SNOWMAN MELT

A HOT-WATER BOTTLE, CAREFULLY PLACED, WILL MELT A SNOWMAN VERY QUICKLY. THE WITCH CAUSING THE FASTEST 'MELT' IS THE WINNER.

SNITCH THE FAIRY

IN THIS GAME, THE WITCH WHO SNITCHES THE MOST CHRISTMAS TREE FAIRIES IS THE WINNER. THE USE OF A BROOMSTICK IS ALLOWED.

LEMON CAROLS

THE MOST BEAUTIFUL CAROL CONCERT CAN BE RUINED BY THE SIGHT OF A WITCH SUCKING A LEMON. THE WITCH SPOILING THE MOST CAROLS WINS.

PRESENT SWAP

A FEW MINUTES SPENT WITH SCISSORS AND STICKY TAPE AMONGST THE PILE OF PRESENTS CAN CAUSE MERRIMENT. NO WINNERS, JUST FUN TO WATCH.

CHAPTER 11
THE MODERN WITCH

91

SUITABLE JOBS

These days witches are seldom required to perform magic for payment and so must earn their living in some other way.

Although the professions shown here employ the sweetest of people they are also a perfect way for the witch to use her talents. The bat ratings show the qualities needed in each job. There are, of course, many more very good opportunities and the determined witch will have no trouble in seeking them out.

AIR STEWARDESS

KEEP FIT INSTRUCTOR

BAT RATINGS

ABILITY TO IGNORE	🦇
DISLIKE OF CHILDREN	🦇
GREED	🦇
MEANNESS	🦇
LUST FOR POWER	🦇
NOSINESS	🦇
STUBBORNNESS	🦇

TELEPHONIST

TRAFFIC WARDEN

92

RECEPTIONIST

SHOP ASSISTANT

TEACHER

TOUR GUIDE

USHERETTE

WAITRESS

INDEX